Heartbeat and Healing

Mental Balance to Academic Success

Aysha Kuhlor MSN, RN, PAC-NE

This journal belongs to _____

Date _____

Daily Self Affirmations
- I am confident in my abilities and trust in my skills to succeed.
- I am resilient and can handle whatever challenges come my way.
- I am constantly learning and growing, becoming a better version of myself every day.
- I am worthy of success and happiness, and I embrace them fully.
- I am grateful for all the positive things in my life and look forward to each new day.

I'm special, I'm beautiful, I'm talented, I'm loved.
I'm _____

I _____

can _____

By the end of the year, I will

Table of Contents

About the Author 5
Foreword 7
Overview 9
Week 1 11
Week 2 13
Week 3 15
Week 4 17
Week 5 19
Week 6 21
Week 7 23
Week 8 25
Week 9 27
Week 10 29
Week 11 31
Week 12 33
Week 13 35
Week 14 37
Week 15 39
Week 16 41
Week 17 43
Week 18 45
Week 19 47
Week 20 49
Week 21 51
Week 22 53
Week 23 55
Week 24 57
Week 25 59
Week 26 61
Week 27 63
Week 28 66
Week 29 68
Week 30 70

Week 31	72
Week 32	74
Week 33	76
Week 34	78
Week 35	80
Week 36	82
Week 37	84
Week 38	86
Week 39	88
Week 40	90
Week 41	92
Week 42	94
Week 43	96
Week 44	98
Week 45	100
Week 46	102
Week 47	104
Week 48	106
Week 49	108
Week 50	110
Week 51	112
Week 52	114

About the Author

As a parent and a nurse, I've navigated the complex terrains of nurturing, healing, and guiding. It's from this dual perspective of caring for both my own children and the numerous individuals who have crossed my professional path that I write this journal.

In our journey through life, particularly during the transformative college years, maintaining balance between mental well-being and academic success is crucial yet challenging. It is a balance that I, as a parent, constantly strive to instill in my children. And it is a balance that I, as a nurse, endeavor to support in my patients.

The journey of a student is often marked by a series of highs and lows. The excitement of new experiences and the pursuit of dreams can sometimes be overshadowed by the pressures of academic success and the navigation of personal challenges. As a nurse, I've witnessed the tangible effects that stress, anxiety, and lifestyle changes can have on one's physical and mental health. And as a parent, I've experienced the deep-seated desire to protect, guide, and provide the best possible foundation for my children as they embark on their own unique paths.

This is why "Heartbeats and Healing: Navigating Mental Balance and Success for Students – College Edition" is more than just a guide; it's a compass for students navigating the complexities of college life. It's a resource I wish had been available for my own children and for the many young individuals I've cared for in my professional life.

This journal, with its weekly insights, activities, prayers and reflections, is designed to equip students with the tools they need to manage stress, cultivate healthy habits, and achieve academic success while maintaining mental balance. It's a guide that acknowledges the challenges and uncertainties of college life but also highlights the opportunities for growth, learning, and self-discovery.

As you embark on this 52-week journey, remember that the path to success is not linear. There will be setbacks and challenges, but there will also be victories and moments of joy. Embrace each experience as an opportunity to learn and grow. And know that in your pursuit of academic and personal development, you are not alone.

To all the students who are about to embark on this journey: I encourage you to approach each week with an open heart and a willing mind. Reflect, engage, and take proactive steps to drive a successful college experience.

Foreword

My college years were a journey through peaks and valleys, marked by struggles with anxiety, depression, and isolation. These challenges, while daunting, shaped my understanding of the importance of mental balance, particularly during the transformative years of higher education.

College life, meant to be an exciting venture into independence and learning, quickly became an overwhelming experience for me. Anxiety would often paralyze my ability to engage with my studies and social environments, while depression would cast a shadow over my achievements and aspirations. Isolation became a defense mechanism, a way to shield myself from the perceived judgment and expectations of the world around me.

However, amidst these struggles, I discovered a powerful tool: journaling. This simple act of self-reflection and expression became my sanctuary, a place where I could confront my fears, acknowledge my feelings, and celebrate my successes, no matter how small.

"Heartbeats and Healing: Mental Balance and Academic Success mirrors the therapeutic journey I embarked upon through journaling. This guide is structured to provide weekly insights and activities, much like the entries in my own journal that guided me through my darkest times. It offers practical steps to manage stress, cultivate healthy habits, and foster a positive mindset, all while navigating the academic and personal challenges of college life.

This 52-week journey is more than just a guide; it's a companion for those who find themselves facing the same battles I once did. It encourages reflection, promotes self-awareness, and provides a structured path to not only confront but also overcome the hurdles of college life.

Through the pages of this journal, I was able to chart a course from struggle to success. It helped keep me on track, reminding me of my strengths and the support systems available to me. Most importantly, it taught me that while facing mental health challenges can be part of the college experience, they do not define nor confine us.

To all the students who may see their reflections in my story, know that you are not alone. This guide is a testament to the strength within you and the potential for transformation and success that lies ahead.

With hope and solidarity,
Kennetra Smith (Student)

Overview

Introduction to Mental Balance and Academic Success

Mental Balance is a crucial component of overall well-being that significantly influences academic success. The relationship between mental health and academic performance is deeply interconnected, with each affecting the other in profound ways.

1. Improved Focus and Concentration
Good mental health enables students to focus better and concentrate on their studies. It reduces distractions caused by anxiety, stress, or depression, allowing students to absorb and retain information more effectively.

2. Enhanced Academic Performance
Students who maintain good mental balance are more likely to perform better academically. Mental well-being helps in managing the pressures of coursework, exams, and deadlines, leading to higher grades and academic achievements.

3. Better Stress Management
Effective stress management is essential for academic success. Mental health strategies such as mindfulness, exercise, and adequate rest can help students cope with the stress associated with academic demands, reducing burnout, and improving productivity.

4. Positive School Experience
Mental health contributes to a positive educational experience. Students who feel mentally healthy are more likely to engage in school activities, build strong relationships with peers and teachers, and develop a sense of belonging within the academic community.

5. Long-Term Benefits
Maintaining good mental balance during the academic years lays a foundation for future success. Skills learned to manage mental health challenges can benefit students in their professional lives, contributing to sustained productivity and job satisfaction.

Conclusion
In summary, mental balance is integral to academic success. By prioritizing mental well-being, students can enhance their focus, manage stress effectively, and achieve higher academic performance. Educational institutions and support systems play a vital role in fostering environments that promote mental health, thereby supporting students' overall success and long-term well-being.

Week 1

Date:

Importance of Mental Balance and Academic Success

Understand the Connection Between Mental Health and Academic Performance
- Research and Discussion: Read articles and watch videos that explain the connection between mental health and academic performance.
- Personal Reflection: Reflect on how your mental health has impacted your academic performance in the past.

Overview of the Series and What to Expect
- Series Outline: Review the topics that will be covered in this series.
- Set Personal Goals: Set personal goals for what you hope to achieve from participating in this series.

Reflect on Understanding
- Journal Reflection: Write about your initial thoughts on the connection between mental health and academic success.
- Set Intentions: Note down what you aim to get out of this series and any specific areas of focus for yourself.

Prayer for Gratitude
"I am grateful for the blessings in my life. May I always recognize and appreciate the abundance around me. Help me to express my gratitude through my actions and

words, bringing positivity and kindness to others."

My Reflection and Goals:

_____

_____

_____

_____

_____

Resources for week 1:
- Articles:
  - "The Connection Between Mental Health and Academic Success" (Psychology Today)
  - "How Mental Health Affects Academic Performance" (National Alliance on Mental Illness)
- Videos:
  - "Mental Health and Academic Success" (YouTube)
  - TED Talk: "The Power of Vulnerability" by Brené Brown
- Books:
  - "Mind Over Mood" by Dennis Greenberger and Christine Pade

Week 2

Date:

Setting Realistic Academic Goals

How to Set Achievable Goals
- SMART Goals Workshop: Participate in a workshop on creating SMART (Specific, Measurable, Achievable, Relevant, Time-bound) goals.
- Create Goals: Draft your academic goals for the semester using the SMART criteria.

Importance of Flexibility and Adapting to Changes
- Flexibility Scenarios: Review case studies or scenarios demonstrating the necessity of adapting goals.
- Discussion Groups: Discuss with peers how to stay flexible with goals in the face of unexpected challenges.

Reflect on Goals
- Goal Setting Reflection: Reflect on the goals you've set and how achievable they feel.
- Adjust and Adapt: Plan for ways to remain flexible and adapt your goals as needed.

Prayer for Strength
"Grant me the strength to face the challenges that come my way. Help me to find resilience within myself and to approach each day with courage and determination. May I be a source of strength for others in need."

My Reflection and Goals:

_____

_____

_____

_____

_____

Resources:
- Workshops:
    - Online SMART Goals Workshops (Coursera, Udemy)
- Templates:
    - SMART Goals Worksheet (Printable)
- Apps:
    - Todoist
    - Trello

Week 3

Date:

The Importance of Routine

Create a Daily Schedule
- Scheduling Tools: Use tools like planners or apps to create a daily schedule that includes time for sleep, meals, exercise, and study.
- Follow the Schedule: Commit to following this schedule for one week.

Identify Improvements and Adjustments
- Routine Journal: Keep a journal of how the schedule affects your productivity and well-being.
- Feedback Session: Share your schedule with peers and get feedback on areas for improvement.

Reflect on Routine
- Identify Benefits: Reflect on one area of your routine that improved your day.
- Adjustments Needed: Identify one area that needs adjustment and plan changes for the next week.

Prayer for Peace
"May peace fill my heart and mind. Help me to find tranquility amidst the chaos and to spread calmness to those around me. Let peace guide my thoughts, words, and actions."

My Reflection and Goals:

_____

_____

_____

_____

_____

Resources:
- Articles:
  - "The Power of Routine in Your Daily Life" (Harvard Business Review)
- Apps:
  - Google Calendar
  - Habitica
- Books:
  - "Atomic Habits" by James Clear

Week 4

Date:

Mindfulness and Its Benefits

Practice Five Minutes of Mindfulness Meditation Each Day
- Guided Meditations: Use guided meditation recordings to practice mindfulness each day.
- Try Different Types: Experiment with different types of mindfulness practices to find what works best for you.

Note Changes in Stress or Concentration Levels
- Mindfulness Log: Keep a log of any changes in your stress or concentration levels.
- Adjust Practices: Modify your mindfulness practice based on what you find most effective.

Reflect on Mindfulness
- Stress and Concentration Reflection: Reflect on how mindfulness practices have impacted your stress and concentration.
- Set Mindfulness Goals: Set a goal to increase or deepen your mindfulness practice based on your reflections.

Prayer for Wisdom
"Grant me the wisdom to make thoughtful decisions. Help me to seek knowledge and understanding, and to use my insights for the betterment of myself and others. May wisdom illuminate my path."

My Reflection and Goals:

_____

_____

_____

_____

_____

Resources:
- Guided Meditations:
    - Headspace App
    - Calm App
- Videos:
    - "Mindfulness for Students" (YouTube)
- Books:
    - "The Miracle of Mindfulness" by Thich Nhat Hanh

Week 5

Date:

Dealing with Homesickness

Write a letter or email to someone from home expressing Your Feelings
- Expressive Writing: Write a heartfelt letter to someone from home, sharing your feelings and experiences.
- Connection Activities: Find a local event or club to attend to build connections in your college community.

Reflect on Emotional Connections
- Homesickness Journal: Reflect on the experience of writing the letter and connecting with home.
- Community Engagement: Reflect on the experience of trying something new and building connections in your community.

Reflect on Homesickness
- Emotional Well-Being: Assess how expressing your feelings and engaging in local activities impacted your feelings of homesickness.

Prayer for Guidance
"Grant me guidance in all that I do. Help me to find clarity in my decisions and to follow a path that aligns with my true purpose. May I be open to the signs and wisdom that guide me."

My Reflection and Goals:

_____

_____

_____

_____

_____

Resources:

- Articles:
    - "Coping with Homesickness" (University Counseling Services)
- Support Groups:
    - Online Student Communities (Reddit, Facebook Groups)
- Books:
    - "The Freshman Survival Guide" by Nora Bradbury-Haehl and Bill McGarvey

Week 6

Date:

Time Management Skills

Use a Planner or Digital Tool to Organize Your Tasks
- Organize Tasks: Use a planner or digital tool to schedule all your tasks for the week.
- Prioritize Daily: Review and prioritize your tasks each morning.

Reflect on Task Completion and Planning Strategy
- Completion Review: Reflect on which tasks were completed and which were not at the end of the week.
- Adjust Planning: Adjust your planning strategy based on your reflections.

Reflect on Time Management
- Effectiveness Review: Reflect on the effectiveness of your time management strategy.
- Plan Adjustments: Make necessary adjustments to your planning strategy for better efficiency.

Prayer for Compassion
"May my heart be filled with compassion for others. Help me to understand and empathize with those who are struggling. Let my actions reflect kindness and a willingness to help those in need."

My Reflection and Goals:

_____

_____

_____

_____

Resources:
- Apps:
  - Notion
  - Microsoft Outlook
- Workshops:
  - Time Management Courses (LinkedIn Learning)
- Books:
  - "Getting Things Done" by David Allen

Week 7

Date:

Stress Management Techniques

Identify Main Stressors and Practice Stress-Reduction Techniques
- Identify Stressors: Make a list of your top stressors related to college life.
- Try Techniques: Practice at least two new stress-reduction methods, such as deep breathing or progressive muscle relaxation.

Reflect on Effectiveness of Techniques
- Stress Log: Keep a log to track stress levels and the effectiveness of the techniques you practiced.
- Technique Review: Review which techniques were most effective and consider how to integrate them into your routine.

Reflect on Stress Management
- Stress Reduction: Reflect on how the new techniques affected your stress levels.
- Routine Integration: Plan how to incorporate the most effective techniques into your daily routine.

Prayer for Healing
"May healing touch my body, mind, and spirit. Help me to find the strength to recover from physical and emotional pain. Grant me patience and hope as I journey toward wellness."

My Reflection and Goals:

_____

_____

_____

_____

_____

Resources:
- Techniques:
    - Deep Breathing Exercises (YouTube)
    - Progressive Muscle Relaxation Scripts (University Counseling Centers)
- Apps:
    - Insight Timer
- Books:
    - "The Relaxation and Stress Reduction Workbook" by Martha Davis

Week 8

Date:

The Power of Positive Thinking
Write and Recite Positive Affirmations
- Create Affirmations: Write down three positive affirmations related to your self-worth, abilities, or goals.
- Daily Recitation: Recite these affirmations daily, integrating them into your morning routine.

Reflect on Mood and Thought Patterns
- Affirmation Log: Keep a log to note any shifts in your mood or thought patterns throughout the week.
- Challenge Negative Thoughts: Set a goal to consciously challenge and reframe negative thoughts.

Reflect on Positive Thinking
- Mood Reflection: Reflect on any changes in your mood or thought patterns as a result of practicing positive affirmations.
- Continue Practice: Decide how to continue integrating positive affirmations into your routine.

Prayer for Unity
"May I work towards unity and understanding among all people. Help me to bridge divides and to promote harmony and collaboration. Let my actions foster a sense of community and mutual respect."

My Reflection and Goals:

_____

_____

_____

_____

_____

Resources:
- Articles:
    - "The Science of Positive Thinking" (Psychology Today)
- Apps:
    - ThinkUp
    - Shine
- Books:
    - "The Power of Positive Thinking" by Norman Vincent Peale

Week 9

Date:

Social Networks and Support Systems

Reach Out and Attend Events
- Social Interaction: Reach out to a friend or family member to catch up and participate in a campus event to meet new people.
- Build Support Systems: Identify and engage with support systems available on campus, such as study groups or counseling services.

Reflect on Social Interactions and Set Goals
- Interaction Review: Reflect on the quality of your social interactions and the support you received.
- Set Social Goals: Set goals to enhance or maintain the quality of your social connections.

Reflect on Support Systems
- Support Evaluation: Assess how your support systems are helping you manage stress and improve well-being.
- Plan for Improvement: Make plans to strengthen or expand your support systems.

Prayer for Unity
"May I work towards unity and understanding among all people. Help me to bridge divides and to promote harmony and collaboration. Let my actions foster a sense of community and mutual respect."

My Reflection and Goals:

_____

_____

_____

_____

_____

Resources:
Apps:
Meetup
Bumble BFF
- Campus Resources:
    - Student Counseling Services
    - Academic Support Centers

Books:
"The Art of Socializing" by Clare Walker

Week 10

Date:

Navigating Academic Pressures

Identify Academic Stressors and Create a Plan
- Stress Identification: Identify the biggest sources of academic stress.
- Develop Coping Strategies: Discuss these stressors with a peer or mentor and create a plan to address them.

Reflect on Plan Effectiveness
- Plan Review: Reflect on the effectiveness of your coping plan at the end of the week.
- Adjust Strategies: Adjust your strategies based on what worked and what didn't.

Reflect on Academic Pressures
- Stress Management: Reflect on how your coping strategies have affected your ability to manage academic pressures.
- Strategy Refinement: Plan any necessary refinements to improve stress management.

Prayer for Forgiveness
"Grant me the ability to forgive those who have wronged me, and to seek forgiveness from those I have wronged. Help me to release resentment and to embrace the healing power of forgiveness."

My Reflection and Goals:

_____

_____

_____

_____

_____

Resources:
- Articles:
    - "Managing Academic Stress" (American Psychological Association)
- Workshops:
    - Academic Success Programs (Campus Centers)
- Books:
    - "How to Study Effectively" by Chris Bailey

Week 11

Date:

Understanding and Managing Anxiety

Note Anxiety Triggers and Practice Techniques
- Identify Triggers: Keep a log of situations that trigger anxiety.
- Practice Techniques: Apply deep breathing or grounding techniques when you feel anxious.

Reflect on Anxiety Patterns
- Anxiety Log: Review your anxiety log to identify patterns or common triggers.
- Technique Effectiveness: Reflect on the effectiveness of the techniques in reducing anxiety.

Reflect on Anxiety Management
- Anxiety Patterns: Reflect on any patterns or common triggers identified and how you managed them.
- Plan for Future Management: Develop a plan for using the most effective techniques to manage anxiety in the future.

My Reflection and Goals:

Prayer for Joy
"May joy fill my heart and radiate to those around me. Help me to find happiness in the simple moments and to share my joy with others. Let joy be a constant presence in my life."

Resources:
- Apps:
    - Pacifica
    - WorryTree
- Books:
    - "The Anxiety and Phobia Workbook" by Edmund J. Bourne
- Support Groups:
    - Online Anxiety Support Groups (Anxiety and Depression Association of America)

Week 12

Date:

Combating Loneliness in College

Join Clubs and Spend Time in Communal Areas
- Expand Social Activities: Join a new interest group or club on campus.
- Utilize Communal Spaces: Spend time in communal areas to encourage casual interactions.

Reflect on Feelings of Loneliness and New Connections
- Loneliness Journal: Reflect on any feelings of loneliness and new connections you've made.
- Connection Review: Assess how engaging in new activities and spending time in communal spaces affected your sense of loneliness.

Reflect on Combating Loneliness
- Social Interaction Impact: Reflect on how new social interactions have impacted your feelings of loneliness.
- Plan for Continued Engagement: Plan how to continue engaging in social activities to combat loneliness.

Prayer for Patience
"Grant me patience in times of trial. Help me to remain calm and composed, even when faced with challenges. Let patience guide my actions and interactions with others."

My Reflection and Goals:

_____

_____

_____

_____

_____

Resources:
- Articles:
  - "Overcoming Loneliness in College" (Active Minds)
  - "How to Cope with Loneliness at College" (Verywell Mind)
- Apps:
  - Meetup (for finding local events and groups)
  - Bumble BFF (for making new friends)
- Books:
  - "Loneliness: Human Nature and the Need for Social Connection" by John T. Cacioppo
  - "Connected: The Surprising Power of Our Social Networks and How They Shape Our Lives" by Nicholas A. Christakis and James H. Fowler
- Support Groups:
  - Campus clubs and organizations (check your university's student life or activities office)
  - Online student communities (Reddit, Facebook Groups)

Week 13

Date:

The Importance of Self-Care

Schedule Self-Care Activities
- Identify Activities: Identify activities that reduce stress and promote well-being, such as hobbies, exercise, or relaxation techniques.
- Plan Integration: Use planning tools to integrate self-care practices into your weekly schedule without compromising study time.

Reflect on Self-Care's Impact
- Journal Prompts: Use journal prompts to reflect on how self-care affects your stress levels and academic performance.
- Group Discussions: Participate in group discussions to share self-care strategies and discover new activities that others find helpful.

Prayer for Hope
"May hope fill my heart and mind. Help me to see the light in times of darkness and to hold onto hope when things seem uncertain. Let hope be a beacon that guides me forward."

My Reflection and Goals:

_____

_____

_____

_____

_____

Resources:
- Articles:
  - "Self-Care Tips for College Students" (NAMI)
  - "The Importance of Self-Care" (Psychology Today)
- Apps:
  - Aloe Bud
  - Reflectly
- Books:
  - "The Self-Care Solution" by Jennifer Ashton

Week 14

Date:

Dealing with Procrastination

Identify Reasons for Procrastination
- Self-Assessment Tools: Use self-assessment tools to understand why you procrastinate and which tasks you tend to put off.
- Workshops on Techniques: Attend workshops on techniques to overcome procrastination, such as the Pomodoro Technique or task breakdown.

Reflect on Procrastination Patterns
- Reflective Exercises: Engage in reflective exercises to identify feelings associated with procrastination and satisfaction from task completion.
- Accountability Groups: Join accountability groups where you can check in with peers to stay on track.

Prayer for Love
"May my heart be open to love in all its forms. Help me to love unconditionally and to show love through my actions. Let love be the foundation of my relationships."

My Reflection and Goals:

_____

_____

_____

Resources:
- Articles:
    - "Understanding and Overcoming Procrastination" (Psychology Today)
    - "The Science of Procrastination" (Harvard Business Review)
- Apps:
    - Forest
    - Focus@Will
- Books:
    - "Eat That Frog!" by Brian Tracy

Week 15

Date:

Exploring Personal Interests and Hobbies

Investigate and Pursue New Hobbies
- Discover Resources: Explore resources for discovering new hobbies and local clubs or organizations related to your interests.
- Schedule Pursuit: Schedule time to regularly pursue these interests.

Reflect on Personal Growth
- Growth Reflections: Reflect on how engaging with personal interests contributes to a more balanced life and better mental health.
- Sharing Sessions: Participate in sharing sessions to learn about diverse interests of peers and possibly find common activities.

Prayer for Humility
"Grant me humility in all my endeavors. Help me to recognize my strengths and weaknesses, and to seek growth without pride. Let humility be my guide in interactions with others."

My Reflection and Goals:

_____

_____

_____

_____

_____

Resources:
- Websites:
    - Skillshare
    - Coursera
- Books:
    - "Find Your Passion: 25 Questions You Must Ask Yourself" by Henri Junttila
- Articles:
    - "How to Find a Hobby" (New York Times)

Week 16

Date:

Healthy Eating Habits

Understand Nutrition's Role and Prepare Healthy Meals
- Nutrition Workshops: Attend nutrition workshops focusing on the brain-food connection and how to prepare simple, healthy meals.
- Cooking Challenges: Engage in cooking challenges where you can share healthy meal creations and recipes.

Reflect on Dietary Impact
- Food Diaries: Maintain food diaries to track how changes in diet affect mental clarity, energy levels, and overall mood.
- Discussion Panels: Join discussion panels with nutrition experts to ask questions and seek advice.

Prayer for Acceptance
"May I find acceptance in myself and others. Help me to embrace differences and to understand that each person's journey is unique. Let acceptance bring peace to my heart."

My Reflection and Goals:

_____

_____

_____

_____

_____

Resources:
- Articles:
    - "Nutrition Tips for College Students" (Academy of Nutrition and Dietetics)
    - "Healthy Eating on a Budget" (Harvard T.H. Chan School of Public Health)
- Apps:
    - MyFitnessPal
    - Yummly
- Books:
    - "The College Vegetarian Cookbook" by Stephanie McKercher

Week 17

Date:

Physical Activity and Mental Health

Experiment with Different Physical Activities
- Instructor-Led Activities: Try out various instructor-led physical activities, such as yoga, jogging, or dance.
- Exercise Benefits: Learn how different types of exercise benefit mental health.

Reflect on Exercise and Motivation
- Monitor Exercise: Use tools to monitor exercise frequency and mood changes.
- Exercise Reflection: Reflect on your motivation levels for exercising and how physical activity affects your mental state.

Prayer for Clarity
"Grant me clarity in my thoughts and decisions. Help me to see situations clearly and to make informed choices. Let clarity be my guide in moments of confusion."

My Reflection and Goals:

_____

_____

_____

_____

Resources:
- Apps:
  - Nike Training Club
  - 7 Minute Workout
- Articles:
  - "The Benefits of Physical Activity" (CDC)
  - "Exercise and Mental Health" (Mayo Clinic)
- Books:
  - "Spark: The Revolutionary New Science of Exercise and the Brain" by John J. Ratey

Week 18

Date:

Understanding Depression in College Students

Learn About Depression
- Education Sessions: Attend education sessions on the signs and symptoms of depression in college students.
- Support Plan: Draft a plan on how and when to seek professional help if you or someone you know shows signs of depression.

Reflect on Awareness
- Importance of Recognition: Reflect on the importance of recognizing depression and the value of seeking help.
- Assess Support System: Assess the strength of your support system and consider ways to improve it.

Prayer for Positivity
"May positivity fill my mind and soul. Help me to focus on the good and to spread positivity to those around me. Let positive thoughts and actions shape my life."

My Reflection and Goals:

_____

_____

_____

Resources:
- Articles:
    - "Depression on College Campuses" (National Institute of Mental Health)
    - "College Students and Depression" (Mayo Clinic)
- Support Groups:
    - Depression and Bipolar Support Alliance (DBSA)

Week 19

Date:

Overcoming Social Anxiety

Understand Social Anxiety
- Research Social Anxiety: Educate yourself on social anxiety and its effects on college students.
- Confidence Strategies: Practice strategies to improve social confidence in small, manageable situations.

Reflect on Social Comfort
- Progress Reflection: Reflect on any progress made in social situations and identify areas for improvement.
- Strategy Evaluation: Evaluate the effectiveness of the strategies used and consider continuing or adjusting them.

Prayer for Forgiveness
"Grant me the strength to forgive others and myself. Help me to let go of grudges and to seek reconciliation. Let forgiveness bring healing and peace to my heart."

My Reflection and Goals:

_____

_____

_____

Resources:
- Apps:
  - MindShift (CBT-based app for anxiety)
  - Joyable (guided programs for social anxiety)
- Books:
  - "Overcoming Social Anxiety and Shyness" by Gillian Butler
  - "The Anxiety Toolkit" by Alice Boyes
- Support Groups:
  - Social Anxiety Support Forums (Social Anxiety Association)
  - Meetup groups for social anxiety (meetup.com)
- Articles:
  - "How to Overcome Social Anxiety" (Psychology Today)
  - "Coping with Social Anxiety" (Anxiety and Depression Association of America)

Week 20

Date:

Effective Communication Skills

Study Communication Techniques
- Learn Techniques: Study clear and assertive communication techniques.
- Practice Communication: Apply these techniques in your personal and academic interactions throughout the week.

Reflect on Communication Improvement
- Interaction Reflection: Reflect on how these techniques have affected your interactions with your friends and colleagues.

Prayer for Creativity
"May creativity flow through me. Help me to express myself in unique and meaningful ways. Let creativity be a source of joy and inspiration in my life."

My Reflection and Goals:

_____

_____

_____

_____

_____

Resources:
- Articles:
  - "Effective Communication Skills" (Skills You Need)
  - "The Importance of Effective Communication" (Psychology Today)
- Workshops:
  - Communication Skills Workshops (Campus Career Centers)
- Books:
  - "Crucial Conversations" by Kerry Patterson, Joseph Grenny, Ron McMillan, and Al Switzler
  - "Nonviolent Communication: A Language of Life" by Marshall B. Rosenberg
- Online Courses:
  - Effective Communication Specialization (Coursera)
  - Communication Skills for University Success (edX)

Week 21

Date:

Balancing Work and Study

Time Management for Work-Study Balance
- Implement Techniques: Use time-management techniques to allocate time for part-time work and full-time studies.
- Stress Management: Apply stress management strategies to cope with juggling multiple responsibilities.

Reflect on Balance
- Balance Evaluation: Reflect on your ability to balance work and study effectively.
- Adjust Strategies: Plan any necessary changes to your strategies for maintaining balance.

Prayer for Courage
"Grant me the courage to face my fears. Help me to step out of my comfort zone and to embrace all challenges with courage.

My Reflection and Goals:

_____

_____

_____

_____

Resources:
- Articles:
    - "Balancing Work and Study" (CollegeBoard)
    - "How to Balance Work and School" (Fastweb)
- Apps:
    - TimeTree (shared calendar app)
    - RescueTime (time management and productivity app)
- Books:
    - "The Work-School Balance Guide" by Maria Kodama
    - "How to Have a Good Day" by Caroline Webb
- Workshops:
    - Time management and productivity workshops (offered by campus career centers or online learning platforms)

Week 22

Date:

Building Resilience

Understand Resilience
- Research Resilience: Research the concept of resilience and its importance for mental health.
- Engage in Activities: Participate in activities designed to build and strengthen your resilience.

Reflect on Resilience Growth
- Growth Reflection: Reflect on how the activities have contributed to your resilience.
- Resilience Plan: Plan how you will continue to cultivate resilience in the long term.

Prayer for Balance
"May I find balance in all aspects of my life. Help me to manage my time and energy wisely. Let balance bring harmony and well-being."

My Reflection and Goals:

_____

_____

_____

_____

_____

Resources:
- Articles:
    - "How to Build Resilience" (American Psychological Association)
    - "Resilience: Build Skills to Endure Hardship" (Mayo Clinic)
- Workshops:
    - Resilience Training (Campus Wellness Centers)
- Books:
    - "Resilient: How to Grow an Unshakable Core of Calm, Strength, and Happiness" by Rick Hanson
    - "The Resilience Factor" by Karen Reivich and Andrew Shatté
- Apps:
    - Happify (activities and games for

Week 23

Date:

Navigating Relationship Challenges

Relationship Skills
- Learn Skills: Educate yourself on managing both romantic and platonic relationships effectively.
- Practice Communication: Apply communication skills and boundary-setting in your relationships.

Reflect on Relationship Dynamics
- Dynamics Reflection: Reflect on the dynamics of your relationships and any improvements or challenges faced.
- Healthy Relationships Plan: Decide on strategies you will continue to use or new ones to implement for healthy relationships.

Prayer for Resilience
"May resilience strengthen my spirit. Help me to recover from setbacks and to persevere through difficulties. Let resilience guide me through life's challenges."

My Reflection and Goals:

_____

_____

_____

_____

Resources:
- Articles:
    - "Managing Relationship Challenges" (Psychology Today)
    - "Healthy Relationships" (Loveisrespect.org)
- Support Services:
    - Campus Relationship Counseling (offered by university counseling centers)
    - Online counseling platforms (BetterHelp, Talkspace)
- Books:
    - "The Seven Principles for Making Marriage Work" by John Gottman
    - "Hold Me Tight: Seven Conversations for a Lifetime of Love" by Dr. Sue Johnson
- Workshops:
    - Relationship skills workshops (often available through campus wellness centers or community organizations)

Week 24

Date:

The Impact of Substance Use

Educate Yourself
- Learn Effects: Research the effects of alcohol and drug use on mental and physical health.
- Reflect on Choices: Reflect on your own choices regarding substance use and explore available resources for help if needed.

Reflect on Impact
- Impact Reflection: Consider the role of substances in your life and their impact on your well-being.
- Informed Choices: Commit to making informed choices about substance use going forward.

Prayer for Integrity
"May integrity be the foundation of my actions. Help me to live in alignment with my values and to act with honesty. Let integrity guide my decisions."

My Reflection and Goals:

_____

_____

_____

_____

Resources:
- Articles:
  - "Understanding Substance Use in College" (National Institute on Drug Abuse)
  - "The Effects of Alcohol and Drug Use" (College Drinking Prevention)
- Support Groups:
  - Alcoholics Anonymous (AA)
  - Narcotics Anonymous (NA)
- Books:
  - "Clean: Overcoming Addiction and Ending America's Greatest Tragedy" by David Sheff
  - "In the Realm of Hungry Ghosts: Close Encounters with Addiction" by Gabor Maté
- Websites:
  - SAMHSA (Substance Abuse and Mental Health Services Administration) - provides resources and support for those dealing with substance use issues.

Week 25

Date:

Mindfulness and Relationships

Apply Mindfulness to Relationships
- Mindfulness Techniques: Practice using mindfulness techniques to enhance your relationships, including mindful listening and speaking.
- Daily Mindfulness: Integrate mindfulness practices into your daily interactions with others.

Reflect on Relationship Quality
- Quality Assessment: Reflect on any changes in your relationships due to mindfulness practices.
- Relationship Goals: Based on your reflections, set goals for continuing to improve your relationships with mindfulness.

Prayer for Connection
"Grant me the ability to connect deeply with others. Help me to build meaningful relationships based on trust and respect. Let connection enrich my life."

My Reflection and Goals:

Resources:
- Apps:
  - Headspace (mindfulness and meditation)
  - Calm (mindfulness and relaxation)
- Articles:
  - "Mindfulness in Relationships" (Mindful.org)
  - "How Mindfulness Can Improve Your Relationships" (Psychology Today)
- Books:
  - "The Mindful Path to Self-Compassion" by Christopher Germer
  - "Wherever You Go, There You Are" by Jon Kabat-Zinn
- Workshops:
  - Mindfulness-based relationship enhancement (offered by various wellness centers and online platforms)

Week 26

Date:

Mid-Year Reflection

Reflect on Progress
- Progress Review: Review your academic, personal, and mental health progress thus far.
- Set New Goals: Identify areas for improvement and set new goals for the remainder of the year.

Reflect on Setbacks
- Setback Reflection: Acknowledge any setbacks you've experienced and what you've learned from them.
- Future Success Plan: Create a plan of action for achieving your goals for the second half of the year.

Prayer for Generosity
"Grant me a generous spirit. Help me to give freely of my time, resources, and love. Let generosity bring fulfillment and joy."

My Reflection and Goals:

_____

_____

_____

_____

Resources:
- Templates:
  - Mid-Year Reflection Worksheet (Printable)
  - Reflective Journaling Prompts (Google Docs)
- Apps:
  - Day One Journal (journaling app)
  - Penzu (online journaling platform)
- Books:
  - "The Reflective Journal" by Barbara Bassot
  - "How to Reflect: Improve Your Self-Awareness to Maximize Your Performance" by Jenny Grant Rankin
- Articles:
  - "The Importance of Self-Reflection" (Harvard Business Review)

Week 27

Date:

Coping with Failure and Rejection

Embrace Learning from Failure
- Learning Perspective: Shift your perspective to view failure as a learning opportunity.
- Growth Mindset: Practice strategies to cultivate a growth mindset, such as reflection and resilience-building activities.

Reflect on Growth
- Growth Reflection: Reflect on how you've dealt with any failures or rejections and the growth you've experienced.
- Future Challenges Plan: Determine how you will approach future challenges with a growth mindset.

Prayer for Mindfulness
"Grant me mindfulness in every moment. Help me to be present and fully engaged in life. Let mindfulness bring clarity and peace."

My Reflection and Goals:

_____
_____
_____

Resources:
- Articles:
    - "Coping with Failure and Rejection" (Psychology Today)
    - "How to Overcome Failure" (Verywell Mind)
    - "Dealing with Rejection and Building Resilience" (Harvard Business Review)
- Books:
    - "Failing Forward: Turning Mistakes into Stepping Stones for Success" by John C. Maxwell
    - "Option B: Facing Adversity, Building Resilience, and Finding Joy" by Sheryl Sandberg and Adam Grant
    - "The Gifts of Imperfection" by Brené Brown
- Support Groups:
    - Online Support Communities (Reddit, Facebook Groups)
    - Peer support groups (available through campus counseling centers)
- Videos:
    - TED Talk: "The Gift and Power of Emotional Courage" by Susan David
    - TED Talk: "Grit: The Power of Passion and Perseverance" by Angela Lee Duckworth
- Workshops:
    - Resilience-building workshops (offered

by campus counseling or wellness centers)
- Personal development courses on dealing with failure (Coursera, LinkedIn Learning)

Week 28

Date:

Summer Wellness Tips

Plan Summer Activities
- Wellness Activities: Plan activities that contribute to both mental and physical wellness during the summer.
- Routine Adjustment: Adjust your routine to incorporate these wellness activities.

Reflect on Wellness Impact
- Impact Reflection: Reflect on how engaging in summer activities affects your overall well-being.
- Summer Wellness Plan: Decide how you will continue to incorporate wellness activities throughout the summer.

Prayer for Understanding
"May understanding fill my heart and mind. Help me to listen with empathy and to seek to understand others. Let understanding foster compassion."

My Reflection and Goals:

_____

_____

_____

_____

Resources:
- Articles:
    - "Coping with Failure and Rejection" (Psychology Today)
    - "How to Overcome Failure" (Verywell Mind)
- Books:
    - "Failing Forward: Turning Mistakes into Stepping Stones for Success" by John C. Maxwell
    - "Option B: Facing Adversity, Building Resilience, and Finding Joy" by Sheryl Sandberg and Adam Grant
- Support Groups:
    - Online Support Communities (Reddit, Facebook Groups)

Week 29

Date:

Preparing for the New Semester

Set Intentions and Goals
- Goals Outline: Outline your intentions and goals for the upcoming semester.
- Organize Space and Schedule: Prepare your physical and digital space for the new semester and create a preliminary schedule.

Reflect on Preparedness
- Preparedness Reflection: Reflect on how prepared you feel for the new semester after organizing and setting goals.
- Adjustments Plan: Consider if any further adjustments are needed to your space, schedule, or goals.

Prayer for Wisdom
"Grant me wisdom to navigate life's complexities. Help me to learn from experiences and to make wise choices. Let wisdom illuminate my path."

My Reflection and Goals:

_____

_____

_____

_____

_____

Resources:
- Templates:
    - Semester Planning Worksheet (Printable)
    - Weekly Planner Templates (Google Docs)
- Apps:
    - Notion
    - Google Calendar
- Books:
    - "The Organized Student" by Donna Goldberg

Week 30

Date:

Mindful Reading and Learning

Practice Mindful Reading
- Mindful Techniques: Apply mindfulness techniques to enhance reading comprehension and retention.
- Study Strategies: Experiment with different study strategies to find the most effective one's for you.

Reflect on Comprehension
- Comprehension Reflection: Reflect on how mindfulness has affected your comprehension and retention of study material.
- Strategy Evaluation: Evaluate which study strategies worked best for you and plan to continue using them.

Prayer for Joy
"May joy be ever-present in my life. Help me to find happiness in small moments and to share joy with others. Let joy be a source of strength."

My Reflection and Goals:

_____

_____

_____

_____

_____

Resources:
- Articles:
    - "Mindful Reading Techniques" (Mindful.org)
    - "Improving Learning through Mindfulness" (Harvard Business Review)
- Apps:
    - Kindle with X-Ray feature
    - Readwise
- Books:
    - "The Mindful Scholar" by David M. Levy

Week 31

Date:

Conflict Resolution Skills

Identify Conflict Sources
- Reflect on Conflicts: Reflect on recent conflicts and identify their sources.
- Resolution Strategies: Apply conflict resolution strategies to address any current conflicts effectively.

Reflect on Conflict Management
- Management Reflection: Reflect on how well you managed conflicts during the week.
- Strategy Adjustment: Decide if you need to adjust your conflict resolution strategies for future use.

Prayer for Healing
"Grant me healing in body, mind, and spirit. Help me to find the strength to overcome pain and to seek wholeness. Let healing bring peace and renewal."

My Reflection and Goals:

_____

_____

_____

_____

Resources:
- Articles:
  - "Conflict Resolution Skills" (Skills You Need)
  - "Managing and Resolving Conflict in Relationships" (HelpGuide)
- Workshops:
  - Conflict Resolution Workshops (Campus Mediation Centers)
- Books:
  - "The Conflict Resolution Toolbox" by Gary T. Furlong

Week 32

Date:

The Role of Creativity in Mental Health

Explore Creative Outlets
- Creative Activities: Identify creative activities that you enjoy or have wanted to try, and engage in one this week.
- Daily Creativity: Find ways to include small acts of creativity into your everyday routine.

Reflect on Creativity's Impact
- Stress Reflection: Reflect on how creativity has influenced your stress levels and overall mental health.
- Creative Expression Plan: Consider how you will continue to make space for creative expression in your life.

Prayer for Justice
"May justice guide my actions. Help me to stand up for what is right and to support fairness. Let justice create a more equitable world."

My Reflection and Goals:

_____

_____

_____

_____

_____

Resources:
- Articles:
    - "The Connection Between Art, Healing, and Public Health" (American Journal of Public Health)
    - "How Creativity Positively Impacts Your Health" (Forbes)
- Apps:
    - Procreate (for digital art)
    - Adobe Spark
- Books:
    - "The Artist's Way" by Julia Cameron

Week 33

Date:

Sleep Hygiene for Students

Learn About Sleep Hygiene
- Research Practices: Educate yourself on the best practices for sleep hygiene tailored to student life.
- Implement Habits: Adopt new sleep habits to improve your sleep quality, such as setting a regular bedtime and creating a calming pre-sleep routine.

Reflect on Sleep Quality
- Sleep Journal: Keep a sleep journal to track changes in your sleep quality and duration.
- Routine Adjustment: Reflect on any improvements and adjust your sleep routine as necessary.

Prayer for Peace
"Grant me peace in my heart and mind. Help me to find tranquility in chaos and to spread peace to others. Let peace be my constant companion."

My Reflection and Goals:

_____

_____

_____

_____

_____

Resources:
- Articles:
  - "Sleep Hygiene Tips" (National Sleep Foundation)
  - "How to Improve Your Sleep" (Harvard Medical School)
- Apps:
  - Sleep Cycle (sleep tracking)
  - Calm (sleep stories and meditation)
- Books:
  - "Why We Sleep: Unlocking the Power of Sleep and Dreams" by Matthew Walker

Week 34

Date:

Financial Stress and Management

Financial Planning
- Create a Budget: Develop a budget and explore financial resources available for students.
- Implement Tips: Apply practical budgeting tips to your daily life to help manage your finances.

Reflect on Financial Stress
- Stress Assessment: Reflect on how managing your finances has affected your stress levels.
- Plan Refinement: Adjust your financial plan and budgeting practices based on your reflections.

Prayer for Compassion
"May compassion fill my soul. Help me to feel for others and to act with kindness. Let compassion be a guiding force in my life."

My Reflection and Goals:

_____

_____

_____

_____

_____

Resources:
- Articles:
  - "Managing Financial Stress" (Psychology Today)
  - "Financial Tips for College Students" (NerdWallet)
- Apps:
  - Mint (budgeting and finance app)
  - YNAB (You Need a Budget)
- Books:
  - "I Will Teach You to Be Rich" by Ramit Sethi
  - "The Total Money Makeover" by Dave Ramsey
- Workshops:
  - Financial literacy workshops (offered by campus career services or financial aid offices)
  - Online courses on personal finance (Coursera, Udemy)

Week 35

Date:

The Importance of Gratitude

Gratitude Practices
- Daily Practices: Implement daily practices of gratitude, such as keeping a gratitude journal or expressing thanks to others.
- Reflect on Gratitude: Reflect daily on things you are grateful for and how this practice influences your mental health.

Reflect on Gratitude's Effects
- Mood Reflection: Reflect on how practicing gratitude has affected your mood and outlook.
- Incorporate Gratitude: Decide how you will continue to incorporate gratitude practices into your daily routine.

Prayer for Gratitude
"Grant me a heart full of gratitude. Help me to see the blessings in my life and to express thanks. Let gratitude enrich my soul."

My Reflection and Goals:

_____

_____

_____

_____

_____

Resources:
- Articles:
  - "The Science of Gratitude" (Greater Good Science Center)
  - "Why Gratitude Is Good" (Psychology Today)
- Apps:
  - Gratitude Journal
  - Daylio
- Books:
  - "The Gratitude Diaries" by Janice Kaplan
  - "Thanks! How Practicing Gratitude Can Make You Happier" by Robert Emmons
- Workshops:
  - Gratitude practice workshops (offered by campus wellness centers or online platforms)

Week 36

Date:

Setting Boundaries for Mental Health

Learn About Boundaries
- Educate Yourself: Learn about the importance of setting healthy personal and academic boundaries.
- Implement Boundaries: Practice setting and communicating your boundaries with others.

Reflect on Boundaries
- Effectiveness Reflection: Reflect on how setting boundaries can make you succeed.

Prayer for Self-Compassion
"May I treat myself with kindness and understanding. Help me to be gentle with myself in times of struggle. Let self-compassion nurture my well-being."

My Reflection and Goals:

_____

_____

_____

_____

_____

Resources:
- Articles:
  - "How to Set Healthy Boundaries" (Psychology Today)
  - "The Importance of Setting Boundaries" (Verywell Mind)
- Books:
  - "Boundaries: When to Say Yes, How to Say No to Take Control of Your Life" by Henry Cloud and John Townsend
  - "Set Boundaries, Find Peace: A Guide to Reclaiming Yourself" by Nedra Glover Tawwab
- Workshops:
  - Boundaries workshops (offered by campus counseling centers or wellness programs)
  - Online courses on boundary setting (Skillshare)

Week 37

Date:

Overcoming Imposter Syndrome

Understand Imposter Syndrome
- Research Syndrome: Research imposter syndrome and how it manifests in students.
- Build Confidence: Engage in exercises designed to build self-confidence and confront imposter feelings.

Reflect on Self-Perception
- Perception Reflection: Reflect on any imposter syndrome experiences and your response to confidence-building exercises.
- Plan for Confidence Growth: Determine strategies to continue building confidence in your abilities and combating imposter syndrome.

Prayer for Focus
"Grant me the ability to focus on my goals. Help me to eliminate distractions and to work diligently. Let focus lead to achievement and success."

My Reflection and Goals:

_____

_____

_____

Resources:
- Articles:
  - "Understanding and Overcoming Imposter Syndrome" (Harvard Business Review)
  - "Do You Suffer from Imposter Syndrome?" (Psychology Today)
- Books:
  - "The Secret Thoughts of Successful Women" by Valerie Young
  - "Daring Greatly" by Brené Brown
- Workshops:
  - Imposter Syndrome workshops (offered by campus counseling centers or career services)
  - Online courses on overcoming imposter syndrome (LinkedIn Learning, Coursera)

Week 38

Date:

Self-Expression and Identity

Explore Personal Identity
- Identity Exploration: Take time to explore and express your personal identity through various mediums.
- Engage in Activities: Engage in activities that allow you to express yourself creatively and authentically.

Reflect on Identity and Expression
- Identity Reflection: Reflect on how self-expression activities have helped you understand and articulate your identity.
- Plan for Ongoing Expression: Plan how you will continue to explore and express your identity.

Prayer for Respect
"May I show respect to all beings. Help me to honor the dignity of others and to act with consideration. Let respect build a foundation of trust and harmony."

My Reflection and Goals:

_____

_____

_____

_____

_____

Resources:
- Articles:
    - "The Importance of Self-Expression" (Psychology Today)
    - "Exploring Identity and Self-Expression" (Verywell Mind)
- Books:
    - "The Gifts of Imperfection" by Brené Brown
    - "Braving the Wilderness" by Brené Brown
- Workshops:
    - Self-expression and identity workshops (offered by campus wellness centers)
    - Online courses on personal identity and self-expression (edX, Coursera)

Week 39

Date:

Mental Health Myths Debunked

Educate Yourself
- Debunk Myths: Research and debunk common myths surrounding mental health.
- Share Knowledge: Share what you've learned with peers to promote a more informed perspective on mental health.

Reflect on Misconceptions
- Misconception Reflection: Reflect on how debunking myths has impacted your understanding of mental health.
- Plan for Advocacy: Decide how you will continue to advocate for mental health awareness and education.

Prayer for Renewal
"Grant me renewal in mind, body, and spirit. Help me to rejuvenate and to embrace each new day with energy. Let renewal bring vitality and hope."

My Reflection and Goals:

_____

_____

_____

_____

_____

Resources:
- Articles:
    - "Debunking Mental Health Myths" (National Alliance on Mental Illness)
    - "Common Mental Health Myths and Misconceptions" (Mental Health Foundation)
- Books:
    - "The Man Who Mistook His Wife for a Hat" by Oliver Sacks
    - "Crazy Like Us: The Globalization of the American Psyche" by Ethan Watters
- Websites:
    - NAMI (National Alliance on Mental Illness)
    - Mental Health America
- Workshops:
    - Mental health awareness workshops (offered by campus counseling centers)
    - Online courses on mental health literacy (Coursera, FutureLearn)

Week 40

Date:

Planning for Life After College

Post-College Planning
- Career Planning: Begin planning for your life after college, considering career, living situation, and continued education.
- Resource Gathering: Collect resources and information that will assist in your transition from college to post-graduate life.

Reflect on Preparedness
- Preparedness Reflection: Reflect on your preparedness for life after college and identify any areas of uncertainty.
- Transition Plan: Develop a detailed plan to address any uncertainties and ensure a smooth transition to post-college life.

Prayer for Inspiration
"May inspiration flow through me. Help me to find creative solutions and to express my unique gifts. Let inspiration lead to innovation and joy."

My Reflection and Goals:

___

___

_____

_____

_____

Resources:
- Articles:
    - "Preparing for Life After College" (College Board)
    - "Planning Your Post-College Life" (The Balance Careers)
- Books:
    - "Life After College: The Complete Guide to Getting What You Want" by Jenny Blake
    - "The Defining Decade: Why Your Twenties Matter—And How to Make the Most of Them Now" by Meg Jay
- Websites:
    - LinkedIn Learning (career planning courses)
    - Idealist (career and volunteer opportunities)

Week 41

Date:

Enhancing Academic Engagement

Active Participation
- Class Participation: Commit to actively participating in class discussions and activities.
- Seek Resources: Identify and utilize additional academic resources such as tutoring centers, libraries, or online forums.

Reflect on Engagement
- Engagement Reflection: At the end of the week, assess how these actions have affected your engagement and understanding of the material.
- Plan for Continued Engagement: Decide how you will maintain or increase your level of academic engagement going forward.

Prayer for Self-Acceptance
"Grant me the ability to accept myself as I am. Help me to recognize my worth and to embrace my imperfections. Let self-acceptance bring peace and confidence."

My Reflection and Goals:

_____

_____

_____

_____

_____

Resources:
- Articles:
    - "How to Increase Student Engagement in the Classroom" (Edutopia)
    - "Active Learning Strategies" (Vanderbilt University Center for Teaching)
- Books:
    - "Make It Stick: The Science of Successful Learning" by Peter C. Brown
    - "The Student Engagement Handbook" by Elisabeth Dunne and Derfel Owen

Week 42

Date:

Mastering Study-Life Balance

Audit Time
- Time Audit: Conduct a time audit to see where your time is going, both in studying and personal life.
- Create Balance: Implement strategies to create a better study-life balance, ensuring adequate time for relaxation and hobbies.

Reflect on Balance
- Balance Assessment: Evaluate the effectiveness of your new balance at the end of the week.
- Plan Adjustments: Based on your assessment, plan any adjustments to improve balance for the upcoming weeks.

Prayer for Freedom from Worry
"May I be free from unnecessary worry. Help me to trust in the process and to live in the present moment. Let freedom from worry bring peace of mind.

My Reflection and Goals:

_____

_____

_____

_____

_____

Resources:
- Articles:
    - "Balancing Work and Study" (College Board)
    - "How to Balance School and Life" (The Princeton Review)
- Books:
    - "The Productivity Project: Accomplishing More by Managing Your Time, Attention, and Energy" by Chris Bailey
    - "Essentialism: The Disciplined Pursuit of Less" by Greg McKeown
- Apps:
    - Trello (task management)
    - RescueTime (time management)
- Workshops:
    - Time management and productivity workshops (offered by campus academic support centers or online platforms)

Week 43

Date:

Advanced Note-Taking Strategies

Explore Strategies
- Research Strategies: Research and try out advanced note-taking strategies such as the Cornell method, mind mapping, or the outlining technique.
- Apply a Strategy: Choose one strategy to apply in all your classes for the week.

Reflect on Notetaking
- Evaluate Notetaking: Reflect on how the chosen strategy impacted your comprehension and retention of class material.
- Note-Taking Strategy Decision: Decide if you will continue with the chosen method or experiment with another one.

Prayer for Clarity of Purpose
"Grant me clarity in my life's purpose. Help me to understand my true calling and to pursue it with dedication. Let purpose bring meaning and direction to my days."

My Reflection and Goals:

_____

_____

_____

_____

_____

Resources:
- Articles:
    - "Effective Note-Taking Strategies" (Cornell University)
    - "How to Take Better Notes" (Harvard Extension School)
- Books:
    - "How to Take Smart Notes: One Simple Technique to Boost Writing, Learning and Thinking" by Sönke Ahrens
    - "The Organized Mind: Thinking Straight in the Age of Information Overload" by Daniel J. Levitin
- Apps:
    - Evernote (note-taking)
    - OneNote (Microsoft note-taking app)
- Workshops:
    - Note-taking skills workshops (offered by campus academic support centers)

Week 44

Date:

Personal Branding for Students

Define Your Brand
- Identify Strengths: Begin defining your personal brand by identifying your strengths, values, and goals.
- Online Presence: Update your social media profiles and LinkedIn to reflect your personal brand.

Reflect on Branding
- Brand Reflection: At the end of the week, reflect on how personal branding may impact your future career and networking opportunities.
- Brand Strategy: Plan how you will continue to develop and communicate your personal brand.

Prayer for Joy in Service
"May I find joy in helping others. Help me to serve with a glad heart and to see the impact of my actions. Let joy in service uplift my spirit and those around me."

My Reflection and Goals:

_____

_____

_____

_____

Resources:
- Articles:
  - "How to Build Your Personal Brand in College" (Forbes)
  - "Personal Branding 101" (LinkedIn)
- Books:
  - "Me 2.0: 4 Steps to Building Your Future" by Dan Schawbel
  - "Career Distinction: Stand Out by Building Your Brand" by William Arruda and Kirsten Dixson
- Websites:
  - LinkedIn Learning (courses on personal branding)
  - Canva (tools for creating personal brand assets)
- Workshops:
  - Personal branding workshops (offered by campus career services)

Week 45

Date:

Volunteer Work and Community Service

Research Opportunities
- Find Opportunities: Look for volunteer work or community service opportunities that align with your interests or career goals.
- Participate in Service: Dedicate time this week to participate in a community service or volunteer opportunity.

Reflect on Service
- Service Reflection: Reflect on how community service contributed to your sense of purpose and connection with the community.
- Service Continuation: Decide if and how you will continue to engage in community service regularly.

Prayer for Learning
"Grant me an open mind and a thirst for knowledge. Help me to learn from every experience and to grow wiser each day. Let learning be a continuous journey."

My Reflection and Goals:

_____

_____

_____

_____

_____

Resources:
- Articles:
    - "The Benefits of Volunteering" (Mayo Clinic)
    - "How to Get Involved in Community Service" (The Balance Careers)
- Websites:
    - VolunteerMatch (find volunteer opportunities)
    - Idealist (volunteer and internship listings)
- Books:
    - "The Volunteer Revolution: Unleashing the Power of Everybody" by Bill Hybels
    - "Giving Back: Discover Your Values and Put Them Into Action Through Volunteering and Donating" by Steven Piersanti
- Workshops:
    - Volunteer engagement workshops (offered by campus community service centers)
    - Online courses on the impact of volunteering (edX, Coursera)

Week 46

Date:

Leadership Skills for Students

Leadership Learning
- Learn Skills: Research essential leadership skills and identify which ones you'd like to develop.
- Practice Leadership: Find opportunities in group projects, clubs, or student organizations to practice these skills.

Reflect on Leadership
- Leadership Development: Assess how the practice of leadership skills has impacted your confidence and effectiveness in group settings.
- Future Leadership Goals: Set goals for further developing your leadership abilities.

Prayer for Harmony in Diversity
"May I appreciate the beauty of diversity. Help me to embrace different perspectives and to foster an inclusive environment. Let harmony in diversity enrich my life."

My Reflection and Goals:

_____

_____

_____

_____

Resources:
- Articles:
    - "Developing Leadership Skills in College" (University of Washington)
    - "Leadership Skills for College Students" (Indeed)
- Books:
    - "Leaders Eat Last" by Simon Sinek
    - "The Student Leadership Challenge" by James Kouzes and Barry Posner
- Workshops:
    - Leadership development workshops (often available through campus student life or career services)
    - Online leadership courses (Coursera, LinkedIn Learning)

Week 47

Date:

Digital Literacy and Safety

Educate Yourself
- Learn Practices: Educate yourself on digital literacy, including safe and responsible use of technology.
- Implement Safety: Update your digital practices to enhance security and privacy.

Reflect on Digital Safety
- Safety Evaluation: Reflect on how the changes have impacted your sense of security online.
- Plan for Literacy: Develop a plan for staying informed and practicing digital literacy and safety.

Prayer for Emotional Balance
"Grant me balance in my emotions. Help me to understand and express my feelings in healthy ways. Let emotional balance bring stability and peace."

My Reflection and Goals:

_____

_____

_____

_____

Resources:
- Articles:
    - "Digital Literacy: An Essential Skill for the 21st Century" (Edutopia)
    - "Tips for Staying Safe Online" (National Cyber Security Alliance)
- Books:
    - "The Smart Girl's Guide to Privacy" by Violet Blue
    - "Digital Literacy: A Primer on Media, Identity, and the Evolution of Technology" by Susan Wiesinger
- Workshops:
    - Digital literacy and cybersecurity workshops (offered by campus IT services or online platforms)
- Apps:
    - LastPass (password management)
    - Duo Mobile (two-factor authentication)

Week 48

Date:

Exam Preparation Techniques

Preparation Strategies
- Identify Techniques: Identify and implement effective exam preparation strategies tailored to your learning style.
- Practice Exams: Take practice exams or mock tests to assess your knowledge and readiness.

Reflect on Exam Readiness
- Readiness Reflection: Reflect on your level of preparedness for exams and any anxiety experienced.
- Refinement of Techniques: Decide which preparation techniques worked well and which need refinement.

Prayer for Faith in Humanity
"May I have faith in the goodness of people. Help me to trust and believe in the potential for positive change. Let faith in humanity inspire my actions."

My Reflection and Goals:

_____

_____

_____

_____

_____

Resources:
- Articles:
  - "Effective Study Techniques for Exam Preparation" (Top Universities)
  - "10 Study Tips to Improve Your Learning" (Oxford Learning)
- Books:
  - "How to Study for Exams" by Tony Buzan
  - "Make It Stick: The Science of Successful Learning" by Peter C. Brown
- Workshops:
  - Exam preparation workshops (offered by campus academic support centers)
- Apps:
  - Quizlet (study tools)
  - Anki (flashcard app)

Week 49

Date:

Building Professional Relationships

Networking
- Find Events: Attend networking events or reach out to professionals for informational interviews.
- Follow-Up Routine: Establish a follow-up routine to maintain the professional relationships you've built.

Reflect on Relationships
- Relationship Quality: Evaluate the quality of the connections made and the effectiveness of your communication.
- Networking Goals: Plan how you will continue to build and maintain professional relationships.

Prayer for Inner Peace
"Grant me inner peace that remains steady through life's ups and downs. Help me to cultivate a calm heart and mind. Let inner peace be my sanctuary."

My Reflection and Goals:

_____

_____

_____

_____

Resources:
- Articles:
  - "How to Build Professional Relationships" (The Balance Careers)
  - "Networking Tips for College Students" (NerdWallet)
- Books:
  - "Never Eat Alone: And Other Secrets to Success, One Relationship at a Time" by Keith Ferrazzi
  - "The 20-Minute Networking Meeting" by Marcia Ballinger and Nathan Perez
- Websites:
  - LinkedIn (networking and professional connections)
  - Meetup (professional networking events)

Week 50

Date:

The Role of Mentorship in Personal Growth

Seek a Mentor
- Find Mentors: Look for mentorship opportunities within your field of study or interests.
- Engage with Mentors: Have at least one meeting with a mentor to discuss your academic and professional goals.

Reflect on Mentorship
- Mentorship Impact: Reflect on how mentorship has contributed to your perspective on personal growth and career planning.
- Continued Engagement: Decide how you will continue to engage with your mentor or seek additional mentorship opportunities.

Prayer for Personal Growth
"Grant me the courage to grow and evolve. Help me to embrace change and to see every challenge as an opportunity for growth. Let personal growth lead to self-discovery."

My Reflection and Goals:

_____

_____

_____

_____

_____

Resources:
- Articles:
    - "The Importance of Mentorship" (Forbes)
    - "How to Find and Work with a Mentor" (Harvard Business Review)
- Books:
    - "Lean In: Women, Work, and the Will to Lead" by Sheryl Sandberg (includes a section on mentorship)
    - "Mentoring 101: What Every Leader Needs to Know" by John C. Maxwell
- Websites:
    - MentorNet (mentorship network for students)
    - FindAMentor.com (mentorship opportunities)

Week 51

Date:

Sustainable Living for Students

Learn About Sustainability
- Research Practices: Educate yourself on sustainable living practices.
- Implement Changes: Make one or two changes in your daily routine to live more sustainably, such as reducing waste or conserving energy.

Reflect on Sustainability
- Sustainability Reflection: Reflect on the impact of your sustainability practices on your lifestyle and the environment.
- Sustainability Goals: Plan how you will continue to incorporate sustainability into your life.

Prayer for Empathy
"May my heart be filled with empathy. Help me to understand and share in the feelings of others. Let empathy guide my interactions and build deeper connections."

My Reflection and Goals:

_____

_____

_____

_____

Resources:
- Articles:
    - "Sustainable Living Tips for College Students" (Sierra Club)
    - "10 Ways to Live More Sustainably" (World Wildlife Fund)
- Books:
    - "The Zero Waste Lifestyle" by Amy Korst
    - "Plastic-Free: How I Kicked the Plastic Habit and How You Can Too" by Beth Terry
- Apps:
    - Oroeco (tracks your carbon footprint)
    - GoodGuide (rates products based on health, environment, and social impact)

Week 52

Date:

Year-End Review and Planning

Year-End Review
- Reflect on Progress: Reflect on your academic, personal, and mental health progress over the past year.
- Set New Goals: Set goals for the coming year, building on the insights gained from the past year.

Reflect on Insights
- Review Insights: Identify key learnings from the year-end review that can inform your future.
- Future Planning: Develop a comprehensive plan for achieving your goals in the coming year, considering all the skills and knowledge you've accumulated.

Prayer for Optimism
"May optimism be my outlook on life. Help me to see the best in every situation and to remain hopeful. Let optimism light my path."

My Reflection and Goals:

_____

_____

_____

_____

_____

Resources:
- Templates:
  - Year-End Review Worksheet (Printable)
  - Goal-Setting Templates (Google Docs)
- Apps:
  - Day One Journal (journaling app)
  - Trello (project and goal management)
- Books:
  - "Your Best Year Ever: A 5-Step Plan for Achieving Your Most Important Goals" by Michael Hyatt
  - "The Bullet Journal Method" by Ryder Carroll
- Articles:
  - "How to Conduct a Year-End Review" (Harvard Business Review)
  - "The Importance of Reflecting on Your Year" (Forbes)

Important Phone Numbers for YOU

1. Mom/Dad [.   ]
2. National Suicide Prevention Lifeline: 1-800-273-8255
3. Crisis Text Line: Text "HELLO" to 741741
4. Substance Abuse and Mental Health Services Administration (SAMHSA) National Helpline: 1-800-662-HELP (4357)
5. National Domestic Violence Hotline: 1-800-799-SAFE (7233)

6. National Eating Disorders Association (NEDA) Helpline: 1-800-931-2237
7. Rape, Abuse & Incest National Network (RAINN) Hotline: 1-800-656-HOPE (4673)
8. American Red Cross: 1-800-RED-CROSS (733-2767)
9. Campus Security or Police Department: [   ]
10. University Counseling Center: [   ]
11. Student Health Services: [   ]
12. Financial Aid Office: [   ]
13. Career Services Center: [   ]
14. Local Poison Control Center: 1-800-222-1222
15. LGBTQ+ Youth Helpline (The Trevor Project): 1-866-488-7386
16. Veterans Crisis Line: 1-800-273-8255 (Press 1)

Final Reflection and Conclusion

As you conclude your journey through "Heartbeats and Healing: Mental Balance to Academic Success", it is essential to reflect on the multitude of goals and growth experiences you have explored. This journal has been a guide, a companion, and a source of inspiration, leading you through the intricate dance of academic and mental growth. Take a moment to revisit and reflect on the key areas you've delved into and consider how it has collectively contributed to your holistic development.

Embracing Mental Health for Academic Success
Throughout these weeks, you have come to understand the profound connection between mental health and academic performance. By prioritizing mental well-being,

you set the foundation for resilience, focus, and creativity, all of which are crucial for academic success. Hopefully, this journey has taught you that taking care of your mind is not separate from your educational pursuits; it is integral to them.

Setting Realistic and Achievable Goals
You have learned the importance of setting realistic, achievable goals using the SMART criteria. This practice has helped you to stay focused, motivated, and adaptable in the face of challenges. By breaking down your long-term aspirations into manageable steps, you have created a clear and purposeful path forward.

Cultivating Routine and Balance
Creating and maintaining a balanced routine has been a central theme. You have discovered the significance of allocating time for sleep, meals, exercise, and study, ensuring that each aspect of your life receives the attention it deserves. This balance has fostered a sense of stability and well-being, allowing you to thrive both academically and personally.

Practicing Mindfulness and Self-Care
Mindfulness and self-care have been vital tools in managing stress and enhancing concentration. Through daily mindfulness practices and self-care activities, you have nurtured your mental health and developed a greater sense of self-awareness. These practices have empowered you to stay grounded and present, even amidst the pressures of academic life.

Building Resilience and Coping Strategies
You have explored various coping strategies to deal with

stress, failure, and rejection. By building resilience, you have learned to view setbacks as opportunities for growth and to approach challenges with a positive mindset. This resilience has strengthened your ability to persevere and adapt in the face of adversity.

Fostering Connections and Support Systems
The importance of social connections and support systems has been highlighted throughout your journey. By engaging with peers, mentors, and loved ones, you have created a network of support that enriches your life and provides a sense of belonging. These connections have been a source of encouragement and strength.

Enhancing Personal Growth and Self-Discovery
Self-reflection and personal growth have been recurring themes. You have embraced the journey of self-discovery, exploring your identity, values, and passions. This process has been instrumental in fostering a deeper understanding of yourself and your place in the world.

Practicing Gratitude and Positivity
Gratitude and positivity have been powerful forces in your life. By regularly reflecting on the things, you are thankful for and focusing on positive affirmations, you have cultivated a mindset of appreciation and joy. This practice has enhanced your overall well-being and outlook on life.

Planning for the Future
As you look to the future, you are equipped with the tools and insights gained from this journey. You have learned to plan effectively, set meaningful goals, and navigate the complexities of life with confidence and grace. Your

experiences have prepared you to face the next chapter with optimism and determination.

A Continuous Journey
This journal marks the beginning of a lifelong journey of growth and self-improvement. The practices, reflections, and lessons learned here will continue to guide you as you strive for academic excellence and mental wellness. Carry forward the wisdom and strength you have gained, knowing that every heartbeat and moment of healing contributes to your ongoing journey of personal and academic success.

As we conclude, remember to celebrate your progress, embrace your strengths, and continue to nurture your mental health. Thank you for embarking on this journey with "Heartbeats and Healing". **May your path ahead be filled with growth, joy, and endless possibilities.**

With Gratitude
Aysha

Made in the USA
Middletown, DE
18 September 2024